CHEMISTRY AS A THEORY...

ALL ABOUT ATOMS

S. KAVEEN

Contents

CHAPTER ONE

PRE-17th CENTURY

Prior to the acceptance of the scientific method and its application to the field of chemistry, it is somewhat controversial to consider many of the people listed below as "chemists" in the modern sense of the word. However, the ideas of certain great thinkers, either for their prescience, or for their wide and long-term acceptance, bear listing here.

450 BC

Empedocles asserts that all things are composed of four primal roots (later to be renamed stoicheia or elements): earth, air, fire, and water, whereby two active and opposing cosmic forces, love and strife, act upon these elements, combining and separating them into infinitely varied forms.

440 BC

Leucippus and Democritus propose the idea of the atom, an indivisible particle that all matter is made of. This idea is largely rejected by natural philosophers in favor of the Aristotlean view .

360 BC

Plato coins term 'elements' (stoicheia) and in his dialogue Timaeus, which includes a discussion of the composition of inorganic and organic bodies and is a rudimentary treatise on chemistry, assumes that the minute particle of each element had a special geometric shape: tetrahedron (fire), octahedron (air), icosahedron (water), and cube (earth).

350 BC

Aristotle, expanding on Empedocles, proposes idea of a substance as a combination of matter and form. Describes theory of the Five Elements, fire, water, earth, air, and aether. This theory is largely accepted throughout the western world for over 1000 years.

50 BC

Lucretius publishes De Rerum Natura, a poetic description of the ideas of atomism.

300 BC

Zosimos of Panopolis writes some of the oldest known books on alchemy, which he defines as the study of the composition of waters, movement, growth, embodying and disembodying, drawing the spirits from bodies and bonding the spirits within bodies.

800 BC

The Secret of Creation (Arabic: Sirr al-khalīqa), an anonymous encyclopedic work on natural philosophy falsely attributed to Apollonius of Tyana, records the earliest known version of the long-held theory that all metals are composed of various proportions of sulfur and mercury. This same work also contains the earliest known version of the Emerald Tablet, a compact and cryptic Hermetic text which was still commented upon by Isaac Newton.

850–900 BC

Arabic works attributed to Jābir ibn Ḥayyān (Latin: Geber) introduce a systematic classification of chemical substances, and provide instructions for deriving an inorganic compound (sal ammoniac or ammonium chloride) from organic substances (such as plants, blood, and hair) by chemical means.

900 BC

Muhammad ibn Zakariya ar-Razi (Latin: Rhazes), a Persian alchemist, conducts experiments with the distillation of sal ammoniac (ammonium chloride), vitriols (hydrated sulfates of various metals), and other salts,[13] representing the first step in a long process that would eventually lead to the thirteenth-century discovery of the mineral acids.

1000 BC

Abū al-Rayhān al-Bīrūnī and Avicenna, both Persian philosophers, deny the possibility of the transmutation of metals.

1100–1200 BC

Recipes for the production of aqua ardens ("burning water", i.e., ethanol) by distilling wine with common salt start to appear in a number of Latin alchemical works.

1220 BC

Robert Grosseteste publishes several Aristotelian commentaries where he lays out an early framework for the scientific method.

1250 BC

The works of Taddeo Alderotti (1223–1296) describe a method for concentrating ethanol involving repeated fractional distillation through a water-cooled still, by which an ethanol purity of 90% could be obtained.

1260 BC

St Albertus Magnus discovers arsenic[better source needed] and silver nitrate.[better source needed] He also made one of the first references to sulfuric acid.

1267 BC

Roger Bacon publishes Opus Maius, which among other things, proposes an early form of the scientific method, and contains results of his experiments with gunpowder.[

1310 BC

Pseudo-Geber, an anonymous alchemist who wrote under the name of Geber (i.e., Jābir ibn Hayyān, see above), publishes the Summa perfectionis magisterii, a book containing experimental demonstrations of the corpuscular nature of matter that was still being used by seventeenth-century chemists such as Daniel Sennert. He is one of the first to describe nitric acid, aqua regia, and aqua fortis.

1530 BC

Paracelsus develops the study of iatrochemistry, a subdiscipline of alchemy dedicated to extending life, thus being the roots of the modern pharmaceutical industry. It is also claimed that he is the first to use the word "chemistry".

1597 BC

Andreas Libavius publishes Alchemia, a prototype chemistry textbook.

CHAPTER TWO

17th& 18th CENTURIES

1605

Sir Francis Bacon publishes The Proficience and Advancement of Learning, which contains a description of what would later be known as the scientific method.

1605

Michal Sedziwój publishes the alchemical treatise A New Light of Alchemy which proposed the existence of the "food of life" within air, much later recognized as oxygen.]

1615

Jean Beguin publishes the Tyrocinium Chymicum, an early chemistry textbook, and in it draws the first-ever chemical equation.

1637

René Descartes publishes Discours de la méthode, which contains an outline of the scientific method.

1648

Posthumous publication of the book Ortus medicinae by Jan Baptist van Helmont, which is cited by some as a major transitional work between alchemy and chemistry, and as an important influence on Robert Boyle. The book contains the results of numerous experiments and establishes an early version of the law of conservation of mass.

Title page of The Sceptical Chymist by Robert Boyle (1627–91)

1661

Robert Boyle publishes The Sceptical Chymist, a treatise on the distinction between chemistry and alchemy. It contains some of the earliest modern ideas of atoms, molecules, and chemical reaction, and marks the beginning of the history of modern chemistry.

1662

Robert Boyle proposes Boyle's law, an experimentally based description of the behavior of gases, specifically the relationship between pressure and volume.

1735

Swedish chemist Georg Brandt analyzes a dark blue pigment found in copper ore. Brandt demonstrated that the pigment contained a new element, later named cobalt.

1754

Joseph Black isolates carbon dioxide, which he called "fixed air".

A typical chemical laboratory of the 18th century

1757

Louis Claude Cadet de Gassicourt, while investigating arsenic compounds, creates Cadet's fuming liquid, later discovered to be cacodyl oxide, considered to be the first synthetic organometallic compound.

1758

Joseph Black formulates the concept of latent heat to explain the thermochemistry of phase changes.

1766

Henry Cavendish discovers hydrogen as a colorless, odourless gas that burns and can form an explosive mixture with air.

1773–1774

Carl Wilhelm Scheele and Joseph Priestley independently isolate oxygen, called by Priestley "dephlogisticated air" and Scheele "fire air".

Antoine-Laurent de Lavoisier (1743–94) is considered the "Father of Modern Chemistry".

1778

Antoine Lavoisier, considered "The father of modern chemistry", recognizes and names oxygen, and recognizes its importance and role in combustion.

1787

Antoine Lavoisier publishes Méthode de nomenclature chimique, the first modern system of chemical nomenclature.

1787

Jacques Charles proposes Charles's law, a corollary of Boyle's law, describes relationship between temperature and volume of a gas.

1789

Antoine Lavoisier publishes Traité Élémentaire de Chimie, the first modern chemistry textbook. It is a complete survey of (at that time) modern chemistry, including the first concise definition of the law of conservation of mass, and thus also represents the founding of the discipline of stoichiometry or quantitative chemical analysis.

1797

Joseph Proust proposes the law of definite proportions, which states that elements always combine in small, whole number ratios to form compounds.

1800

Alessandro Volta devises the first chemical battery, thereby founding the discipline of electrochemistry.

CHAPTER THREE

19th CENTURY

1803

John Dalton proposes Dalton's law, which describes relationship between the components in a mixture of gases and the relative pressure each contributes to that of the overall mixture.

1805

Joseph Louis Gay-Lussac discovers that water is composed of two parts hydrogen and one part oxygen by volume.

1808

Joseph Louis Gay-Lussac collects and discovers several chemical and physical properties of air and of other gases, including experimental proofs of Boyle's and Charles's laws, and of relationships between density and composition of gases.

1808

John Dalton publishes New System of Chemical Philosophy, which contains first modern scientific description of the atomic theory, and clear description of the law of multiple proportions.

1808

Jöns Jakob Berzelius publishes Lärbok i Kemien in which he proposes modern chemical symbols and notation, and of the concept of relative atomic weight.

1811

Amedeo Avogadro proposes Avogadro's law, that equal volumes of gases under constant temperature and pressure contain equal number of molecules.

Structural formula of urea

1825

Friedrich Wöhler and Justus von Liebig perform the first confirmed discovery and explanation of isomers, earlier named by Berzelius. Working with cyanic acid and fulminic acid, they correctly deduce that isomerism was caused by differing arrangements of atoms within a molecular structure.

1827

William Prout classifies biomolecules into their modern groupings: carbohydrates, proteins and lipids.

1828

Friedrich Wöhler synthesizes urea, thereby establishing that organic compounds could be produced from inorganic starting materials, disproving the theory of vitalism.

1832

Friedrich Wöhler and Justus von Liebig discover and explain functional groups and radicals in relation to organic chemistry.

1840

Germain Hess proposes Hess's law, an early statement of the law of conservation of energy, which establishes that energy changes in a chemical process depend only on the states of the starting and product materials and not on the specific pathway taken between the two states.

1847

Hermann Kolbe obtains acetic acid from completely inorganic sources, further disproving vitalism.

1848

Lord Kelvin establishes concept of absolute zero, the temperature at which all molecular motion ceases.

1849

Louis Pasteur discovers that the racemic form of tartaric acid is a mixture of the levorotatory and dextrotatory forms, thus clarifying the nature of optical rotation and advancing the field of stereochemistry.

1852

August Beer proposes Beer's law, which explains the relationship between the composition of a mixture and the amount of light it will absorb. Based partly on earlier work by Pierre Bouguer and Johann Heinrich Lambert, it establishes the analytical technique known as spectrophotometry.

1855

Benjamin Silliman, Jr. pioneers methods of petroleum cracking, which makes the entire modern petrochemical industry possible.

1856

William Henry Perkin synthesizes Perkin's mauve, the first synthetic dye. Created as an accidental byproduct of an attempt to create quinine from coal tar. This discovery is the foundation of the dye synthesis industry, one of the earliest successful chemical industries.

1857

Friedrich August Kekulé von Stradonitz proposes that carbon is tetravalent, or forms exactly four chemical bonds.

1859–1860

Gustav Kirchhoff and Robert Bunsen lay the foundations of spectroscopy as a means of chemical analysis, which lead them to the discovery of cesium and rubidium. Other workers soon used the same technique to discover indium, thallium, and helium.

1860

Stanislao Cannizzaro, resurrecting Avogadro's ideas regarding diatomic molecules, compiles a table of atomic weights and presents it at the 1860 Karlsruhe Congress, ending decades of conflicting atomic weights and molecular formulas, and leading to Mendeleev's discovery of the periodic law.

1862

Alexander Parkes exhibits Parkesine, one of the earliest synthetic polymers, at the International Exhibition in London. This discovery formed the foundation of the modern plastics industry.

1862

Alexandre-Emile Béguyer de Chancourtois publishes the telluric helix, an early, three-dimensional version of the periodic table of the elements.

1864

John Newlands proposes the law of octaves, a precursor to the periodic law.

1864

Lothar Meyer develops an early version of the periodic table, with 28 elements organized by valence.

1864

Cato Maximilian Guldberg and Peter Waage, building on Claude Louis Berthollet's ideas, proposed the law of mass action.

1865

Johann Josef Loschmidt determines exact number of molecules in a mole, later named Avogadro's number.

1865

Friedrich August Kekulé von Stradonitz, based partially on the work of Loschmidt and others, establishes structure of benzene as a six carbon ring with alternating single and double bonds.

1865

Adolf von Baeyer begins work on indigo dye, a milestone in modern industrial organic chemistry which revolutionizes the dye industry.

Mendeleev's 1869 Periodic table

1869

Dmitri Mendeleev publishes the first modern periodic table, with the 66 known elements organized by atomic weights. The strength of his table was its ability to accurately predict the properties of as-yet unknown elements.

1873

Jacobus Henricus van 't Hoff and Joseph Achille Le Bel, working independently, develop a model of chemical bonding that explains the chirality experiments of Pasteur and provides a physical cause for optical activity in chiral compounds.

1876

Josiah Willard Gibbs publishes On the Equilibrium of Heterogeneous Substances, a compilation of his work on thermodynamics and physical chemistry which lays out the concept of free energy to explain the physical basis of chemical equilibria.

1877

Ludwig Boltzmann establishes statistical derivations of many important physical and chemical concepts, including entropy, and distributions of molecular velocities in the gas phase.

1883

Svante Arrhenius develops ion theory to explain conductivity in electrolytes.

1884

Jacobus Henricus van 't Hoff publishes Études de Dynamique chimique, a seminal study on chemical kinetics.

1884

Hermann Emil Fischer proposes structure of purine, a key structure in many biomolecules, which he later synthesized in 1898. Also begins work on the chemistry of glucose and related sugars.

1884

Henry Louis Le Chatelier develops Le Chatelier's principle, which explains the response of dynamic chemical equilibria to external stresses.

1885

Eugen Goldstein names the cathode ray, later discovered to be composed of electrons, and the canal ray, later discovered to be positive hydrogen ions that had been stripped of their electrons in a cathode ray tube. These would later be named protons.

1893

Alfred Werner discovers the octahedral structure of cobalt complexes, thus establishing the field of coordination chemistry.

1894–1898

William Ramsay discovers the noble gases, which fill a large and unexpected gap in the periodic table and led to models of chemical bonding.

1897

J. J. Thomson discovers the electron using the cathode ray tube.

1898

Wilhelm Wien demonstrates that canal rays (streams of positive ions) can be deflected by magnetic fields, and that the amount of deflection is proportional to the mass-to-charge ratio. This discovery would lead to the analytical technique known as mass spectrometry.

1898

Maria Sklodowska-Curie and Pierre Curie isolate radium and polonium from pitchblende.

1900

Ernest Rutherford discovers the source of radioactivity as decaying atoms; coins terms for various types of radiation.

CHAPTER FOUR

20th CENTURY

1903

Mikhail Semyonovich Tsvet invents chromatography, an important analytic technique.

1904

Hantaro Nagaoka proposes an early nuclear model of the atom, where electrons orbit a dense massive nucleus.

1905

Fritz Haber and Carl Bosch develop the Haber process for making ammonia from its elements, a milestone in industrial chemistry with deep consequences in agriculture.

1905

Albert Einstein explains Brownian motion in a way that definitively proves atomic theory.

1907

Leo Hendrik Baekeland invents bakelite, one of the first commercially successful plastics.

Robert A. Millikan performed the oil drop experiment.

1909

Robert Millikan measures the charge of individual electrons with unprecedented accuracy through the oil drop experiment, confirming that all electrons have the same charge and mass.

1909

S. P. L. Sørensen invents the pH concept and develops methods for measuring acidity.

1911

Antonius van den Broek proposes the idea that the elements on the periodic table are more properly organized by positive nuclear charge rather than atomic weight.

1911

The first Solvay Conference is held in Brussels, bringing together most of the most prominent scientists of the day. Conferences in physics and chemistry continue to be held periodically to this day.

1911

Ernest Rutherford, Hans Geiger, and Ernest Marsden perform the gold foil experiment, which proves the nuclear model of the atom, with a small, dense, positive nucleus surrounded by a diffuse electron cloud.

1912

William Henry Bragg and William Lawrence Bragg propose Bragg's law and establish the field of X-ray crystallography, an important tool for elucidating the crystal structure of substances.

1912

Peter Debye develops the concept of molecular dipole to describe asymmetric charge distribution in some molecules.

The Bohr model of the atom

1913

Niels Bohr introduces concepts of quantum mechanics to atomic structure by proposing what is now known as the Bohr model of the atom, where electrons exist only in strictly defined orbitals.

1913

Henry Moseley, working from Van den Broek's earlier idea, introduces concept of atomic number to fix inadequacies of Mendeleev's periodic table, which had been based on atomic weight.

1913

Frederick Soddy proposes the concept of isotopes, that elements with the same chemical properties may have differing atomic weights.

1913

J. J. Thomson expanding on the work of Wien, shows that charged subatomic particles can be separated by their mass-to-charge ratio, a technique known as mass spectrometry.

1916

Gilbert N. Lewis publishes "The Atom and the Molecule", the foundation of valence bond theory.

1921

Otto Stern and Walther Gerlach establish concept of quantum mechanical spin in subatomic particles.

1923

Gilbert N. Lewis and Merle Randall publish Thermodynamics and the Free Energy of Chemical Substances, first modern treatise on chemical thermodynamics.

1923

Gilbert N. Lewis develops the electron pair theory of acid/base reactions.

1924

Louis de Broglie introduces the wave-model of atomic structure, based on the ideas of wave–particle duality.

1925

Wolfgang Pauli develops the exclusion principle, which states that no two electrons around a single nucleus may have the same quantum state, as described by four quantum numbers.

$${\displaystyle H(t)|\psi (t)\rangle =i\hbar {\frac {d}{dt}}|\psi (t)\rangle }$$

-The Schrödinger equation

1926

Erwin Schrödinger proposes the Schrödinger equation, which provides a mathematical basis for the wave model of atomic structure.

1927

Werner Heisenberg develops the uncertainty principle which, among other things, explains the mechanics of electron motion around the nucleus.

1927

Fritz London and Walter Heitler apply quantum mechanics to explain covalent bonding in the hydrogen molecule,[108] which marked the birth of quantum chemistry.

1929

Linus Pauling publishes Pauling's rules, which are key principles for the use of X-ray crystallography to deduce molecular structure.

1931

Erich Hückel proposes Hückel's rule, which explains when a planar ring molecule will have aromatic properties.

1931

Harold Urey discovers deuterium by fractionally distilling liquid hydrogen.

1932

James Chadwick discovers the neutron.

1932–1934

Linus Pauling and Robert Mulliken quantify electronegativity, devising the scales that now bear their names.

1935

Wallace Carothers leads a team of chemists at DuPont who invent nylon, one of the most commercially successful synthetic polymers in history.

1937

Carlo Perrier and Emilio Segrè perform the first confirmed synthesis of technetium-97, the first artificially produced element, filling a gap in the periodic table. Though disputed, the element may have been synthesized as early as 1925 by Walter Noddack and others.

1937

Eugene Houdry develops a method of industrial scale catalytic cracking of petroleum, leading to the development of the first modern oil refinery.

1937

Pyotr Kapitsa, John Allen and Don Misener produce supercooled helium-4, the first zero-viscosity superfluid, a substance that displays quantum mechanical properties on a macroscopic scale.

1938

Otto Hahn discovers the process of nuclear fission in uranium and thorium.

1939

Linus Pauling publishes The Nature of the Chemical Bond, a compilation of a decades worth of work on chemical bonding. It is one of the most important modern chemical texts. It explains hybridization theory, covalent bonding and ionic bonding as explained through electronegativity, and resonance as a means to explain, among other things, the structure of benzene.

1940

Edwin McMillan and Philip H. Abelson identify neptunium, the lightest and first synthesized transuranium element, found in the products of uranium fission. McMillan would found a lab at Berkeley that would be involved in the discovery of many new elements and isotopes.

1941

Glenn T. Seaborg takes over McMillan's work creating new atomic nuclei. Pioneers method of neutron capture and later through other nuclear reactions. Would become the principal or co-discoverer of nine new chemical elements, and dozens of new isotopes of existing elements.

1945

Jacob A. Marinsky, Lawrence E. Glendenin, and Charles D. Coryell perform the first confirmed synthesis of Promethium, filling in the last "gap" in the periodic table.

1945–1946

Felix Bloch and Edward Mills Purcell develop the process of nuclear magnetic resonance, an analytical technique important in elucidating structures of molecules, especially in organic chemistry.

1951

Linus Pauling uses X-ray crystallography to deduce the secondary structure of proteins.

1952

Alan Walsh pioneers the field of atomic absorption spectroscopy, an important quantitative spectroscopy method that allows one to measure specific concentrations of a material in a mixture.

1952

Robert Burns Woodward, Geoffrey Wilkinson, and Ernst Otto Fischer discover the structure of ferrocene, one of the founding discoveries of the field of organometallic chemistry.

1953

James D. Watson and Francis Crick propose the structure of DNA, opening the door to the field of molecular biology.

1957

Jens Skou discovers Na^+ /K^+ -ATPase, the first ion-transporting enzyme.

1958

Max Perutz and John Kendrew use X-ray crystallography to elucidate a protein structure, specifically sperm whale myoglobin.

1962

Neil Bartlett synthesizes xenon hexafluoroplatinate, showing for the first time that the noble gases can form chemical compounds.

1962

George Olah observes carbocations via superacid reactions.

1964

Richard R. Ernst performs experiments that will lead to the development of the technique of Fourier transform NMR. This would greatly increase the sensitivity of the technique, and open the door for magnetic resonance imaging or MRI.

1965

Robert Burns Woodward and Roald Hoffmann propose the Woodward–Hoffmann rules, which use the symmetry of molecular orbitals to explain the stereochemistry of chemical reactions.

1966

Hitoshi Nozaki and Ryōji Noyori discovered the first example of asymmetric catalysis (hydrogenation) using a structurally well-defined chiral transition metal complex.

1970

John Pople develops the Gaussian program greatly easing computational chemistry calculations.

1971

Yves Chauvin offered an explanation of the reaction mechanism of olefin metathesis reactions.

1975

Karl Barry Sharpless and group discover a stereoselective oxidation reactions including Sharpless epoxidation, Sharpless asymmetric dihydroxylation, and Sharpless oxyamination.

1985

Harold Kroto, Robert Curl and Richard Smalley discover fullerenes, a class of large carbon molecules superficially resembling the geodesic dome designed by architect R. Buckminster Fuller.

1991

Sumio Iijima uses electron microscopy to discover a type of cylindrical fullerene known as a carbon nanotube, though earlier work had been done in the field as early as 1951. This material is an important component in the field of nanotechnology.

1994

First total synthesis of Taxol by Robert A. Holton and his group.

1995

Eric Cornell and Carl Wieman produce the first Bose–Einstein condensate, a substance that displays quantum mechanical properties on the macroscopic scale.

Printed by Libri Plureos GmbH in Hamburg,
Germany

9 798886 673593